STERLING CHILDREN'S BOOKS
New York

An Imprint of Sterling Publishing Co., Inc.
122 Fifth Avenue
New York, NY 10011

STERLING CHILDREN'S BOOKS and the distinctive Sterling Children's Books logo
are registered trademarks of Sterling Publishing Co., Inc.

© 2020 Buster Books

All rights reserved. No part of this publication may be reproduced, stored in a retrieval system, or transmitted in any form or by any means (including electronic, mechanical, photocopying, recording, or otherwise) without prior written permission from the publisher.

ISBN 978-1-4549-4130-9

For information about custom editions, special sales, and premium and corporate purchases, please contact Sterling Special Sales at 800-805-5489 or specialsales@sterlingpublishing.com.

Manufactured in China
Lot #:
2 4 6 8 10 9 7 5 3 1
07/20

sterlingpublishing.com

Illustrated by Andy Keylock
Cover design by Angie Allison
Interior design by Derrian Bradder
Written by Josephine Southon

ABOUT THIS BOOK

This book is packed with tons of cool trucks to color, from construction vehicles and farm machinery, to super-speed racing trucks and heavy-duty road vehicles.

Next to every picture is a fun fact to discover as you color.

So grab your pens and pencils, fasten your seatbelt, and get ready for a truck-tastic ride!

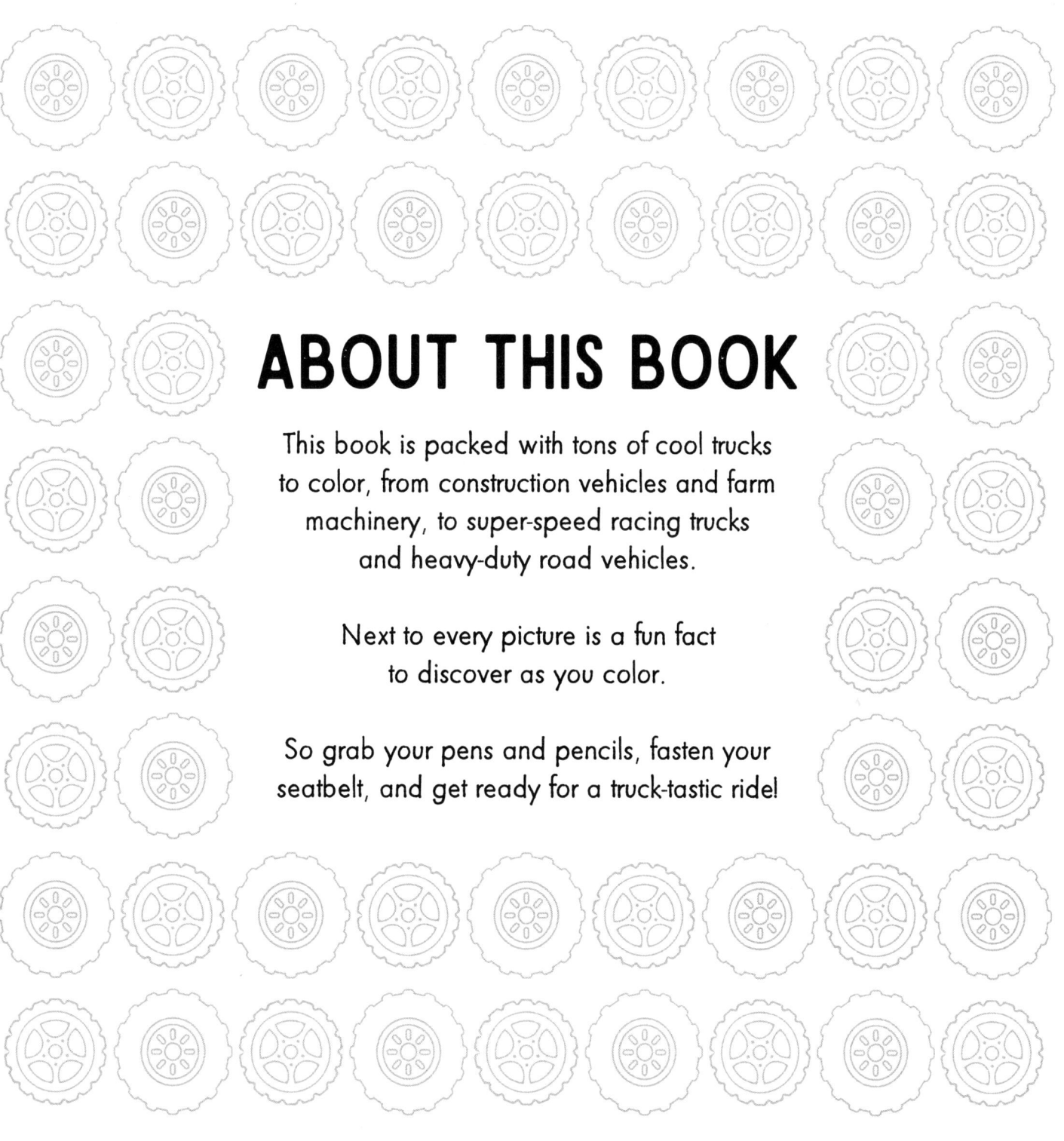

DUMP TRUCK

Dump trucks carry big loads of sand and gravel for use in construction. A pump lifts and tips the box on the back of the truck to unload the material.

WRECKING BALL CRANE

A wrecking ball is a heavy steel ball that is used to knock down buildings. The ball is hung from a crane and swung with incredible force. The heaviest wrecking balls can weigh almost 12,000 pounds (the weight of a monster truck).

TRACTOR

Tractors are used for pulling trailers and farm machinery. The first-ever tractors were powered by steam engines and ran on metal wheels. Today, they run on gasoline, kerosene, and diesel fuel. There are over 16 million of them around the world.

FIRE ENGINE

Fire engines help firefighters get to emergencies quickly. Equipped with everything from ladders and gas masks to medical equipment, these trucks also feature a powerful pump that can spray 1,000 gallons of water per minute (that's enough to fill 20 bathtubs).

SCRAP HANDLER

If metal is thrown away, it can take hundreds of years to break down. However, if it's taken to a scrapyard, it can be recycled and eventually turned into something new. Scrap handlers are used in the yard to move large amounts of metal with their claw-like grabbers.

BIG RIG

Big rigs are also known as semi-trailer trucks or 18-wheelers. The driver sits in the tractor unit, and there can be one or more trailers attached behind for carrying freight. Big rigs can have as many as 18 gears and hold over 200 gallons of fuel. They can weigh over 80,000 pounds – that's 25 times heavier than the average car.

MONSTER TRUCK

The main attraction at motocross events, these flashy trucks can be seen racing around obstacle courses and performing freestyle wheelies and backflips. Some monster trucks are as heavy as 11,900 pounds — the combined weight of 15 grizzly bears. However, this doesn't stop them reaching jumps of more than 30 feet high.

COMBINE HARVESTER

A combine harvester is used to harvest crops such as wheat, oats, and barley. This impressive machine is one of the biggest time- and labor-saving inventions in farming — before it was invented workers picked crops by hand.

SCISSOR LIFT TRUCK

Scissor lift trucks have useful platforms that extend upward, allowing workers to reach high-up places. They are handy on building sites and are also used to maintain buildings and to change light bulbs in streetlights.

FLATBED TRUCK

Big motor vehicles used for transporting heavy loads and goods are called flatbed trucks.

CHERRY PICKER

The cherry picker was first invented in the 1940s to help workers pick hard-to-reach cherries from trees. Today, these trucks are used in maintenance and construction, and by the emergency services.

GARBAGE TRUCK

Did you know that we produce several million tons of trash across the world every day? Garbage trucks help to manage this by transporting the trash to sites where it can be properly disposed of.

DID YOU KNOW?

The longest crane arm in the world is 282 feet long – that's nearly as tall as the Statue of Liberty. The impressive "boom" arm was created by a Chinese manufacturer called SANY.

STEAMROLLER

A steamroller has a wide, heavy wheel for crushing and flattening road surfaces. These tractors used to run on steam, but today they are powered by gas and diesel engines.

TOW TRUCK

The tow truck was first invented in 1916, after someone had to pull a car out of a stream using nothing more than blocks, ropes, and a few friends. Today, you might see tow trucks moving cars from the side of the road when they are damaged or parked in an unsafe spot.

LOGGING TRUCK

When large trees have been cut down in a forest, they are loaded onto a logging truck. The truck transports the logs over long distances to places where they will be used for building houses and furniture, or for making paper.

JET TRUCK

Powered by one or more turbojet engines, these trucks can reach speeds of about 376 miles per hour. One of the fastest trucks in the world, they often compete in runway races against airplanes that fly overhead.

SPIDER EXCAVATOR

This excavator has extendable legs that help it to reach tricky spots and sit on steep or uneven ground. People say it moves like a crab or a spider.

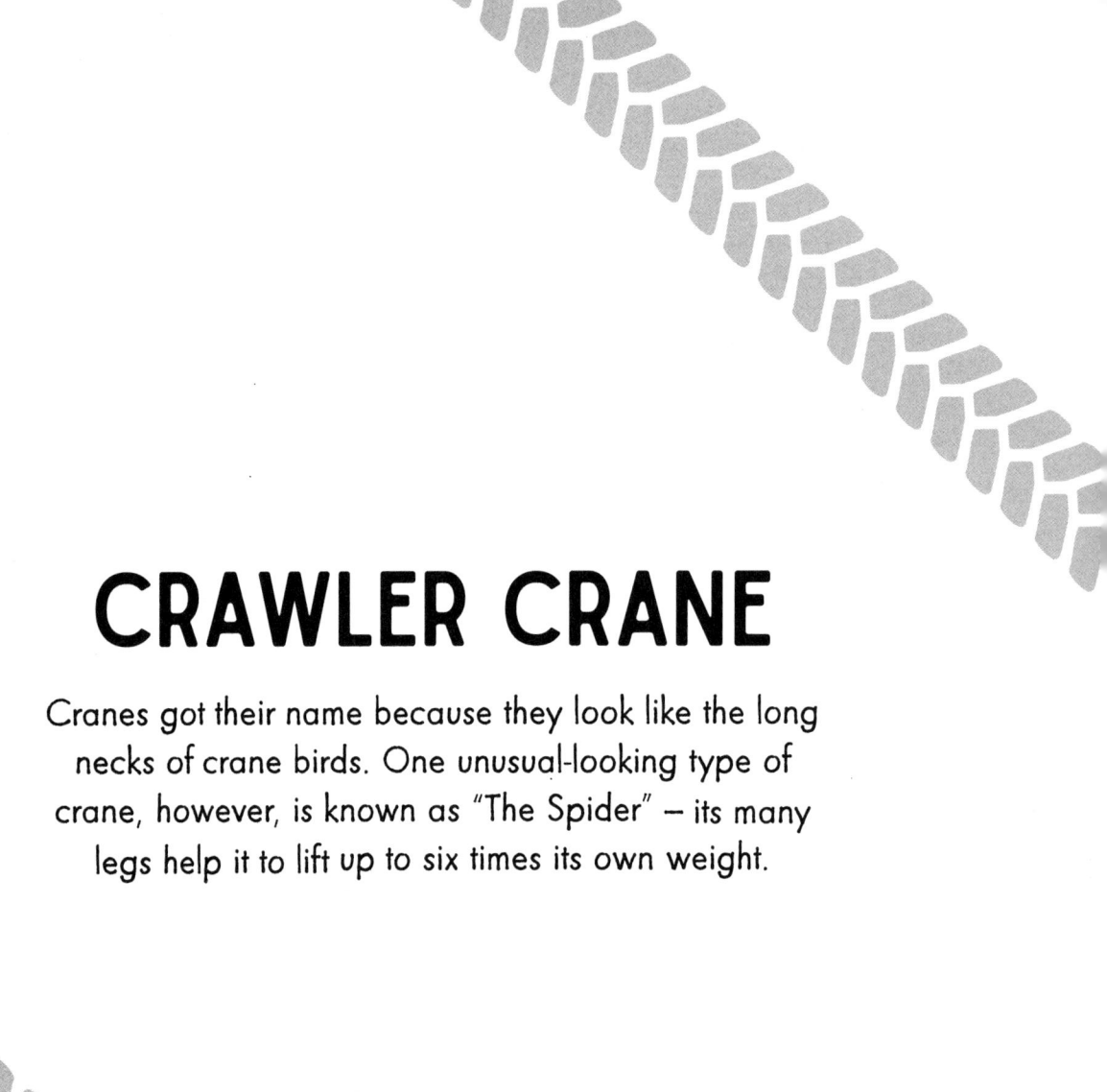

CRAWLER CRANE

Cranes got their name because they look like the long necks of crane birds. One unusual-looking type of crane, however, is known as "The Spider" – its many legs help it to lift up to six times its own weight.

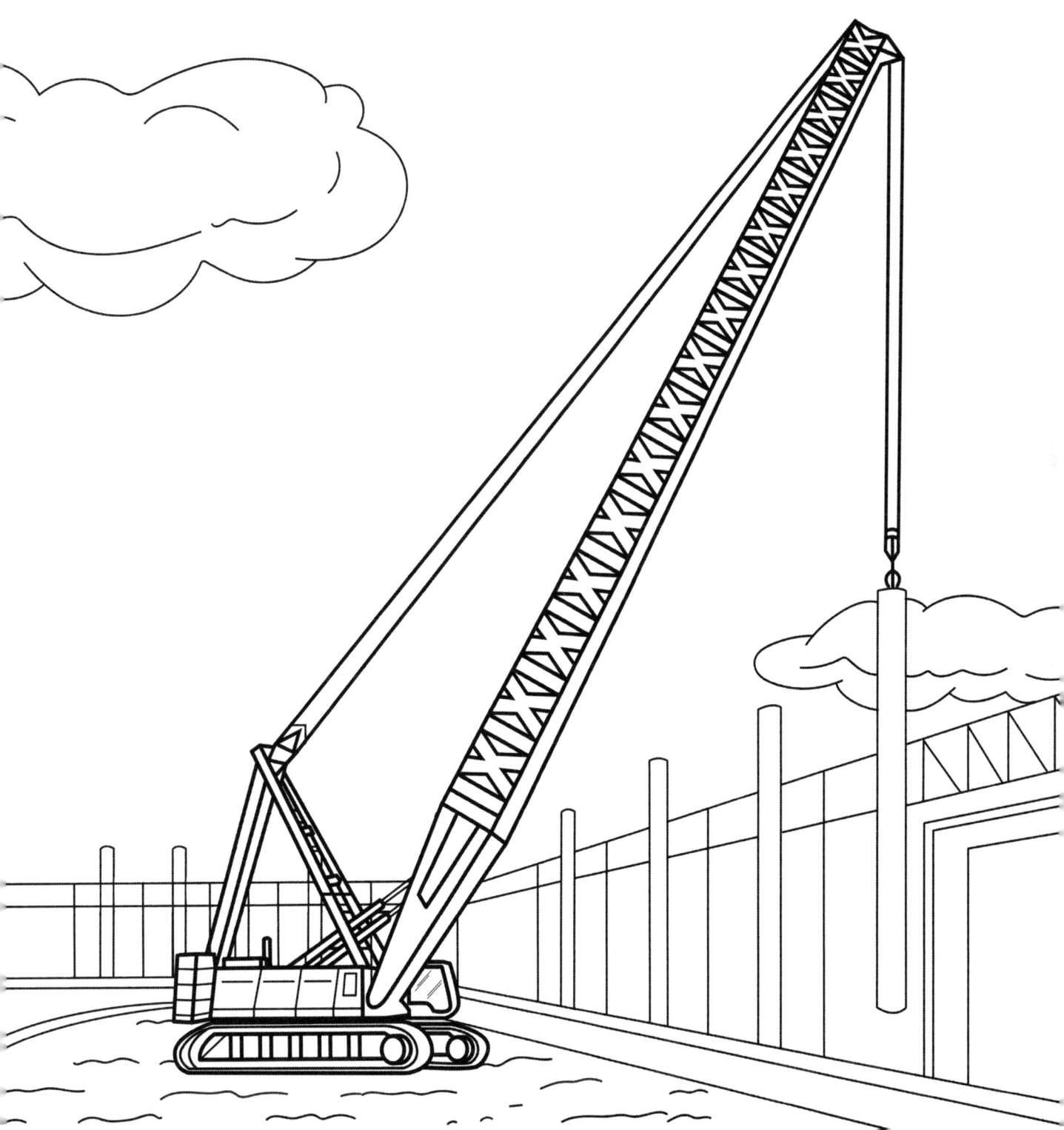

CAR HAULER

Car haulers are used for transporting multiple cars and can carry up to 12 vehicles at once. A ramp at the back of the vehicle allows the cars to be driven on and off the truck easily.

DELIVERY TRUCK

Delivery trucks are used to deliver a huge range of goods, from electrical equipment and furniture, to musical instruments and groceries. Special cold units inside the truck help to keep fridge and freezer food at a perfect temperature.

TRACKED EXCAVATOR

Fitted with wide tracks, these excavators have no problem working on soft or unsteady ground. They are often used for digging large holes, ditches, and basements.

PIPE LAYER

Pipe layers are strong, heavy vehicles that are used to place pipes on construction sites. Despite their size, they also perform well on slopes and on rocky and uneven ground.

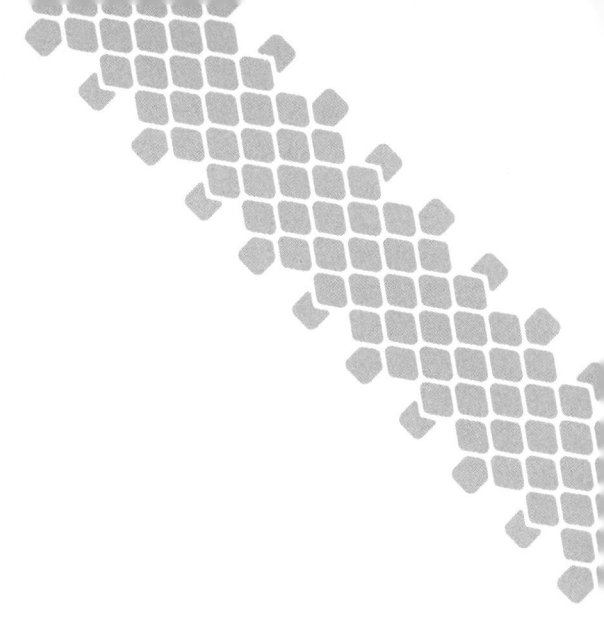

FUEL TANKER

Fuel tankers are used to transport gasoline, oil, gases, and chemicals. Heavy-duty tankers can be filled with over 10,000 gallons of liquid.

BULLDOZER

Bulldozers are fitted with powerful blades at the front to move large amounts of earth and rubble. Their wide tracks help to keep them stable on bumpy ground.

JEEP

The jeep was first developed for the US military to drive on rough ground and in challenging environments. Today, jeeps are also known as SUVs (Sport Utility Vehicles) and are popular for both on- and off-road driving.

LOW LOADER

Low loaders are heavy-duty vehicles used for transporting large vehicles and equipment. The truck's trailer deck is much lower to the ground than a standard trailer, which makes it easier for workers to load and unload heavy machinery.

SNOW COACH

Snow coaches are used in Canada and the United States for driving tourists across the snow-covered landscapes. In the past, these coaches were fitted with skis at the front and rubber tracks at the back. Today, they are fully fitted with either large tires or tracks.

STREET SWEEPER

These trucks are used to suck up trash from city streets and keep them clean. The vehicle was invented in the 1840s in Manchester, England's first industrial city, after it was claimed to be the unhealthiest place to live in the country.

HAUL TRUCK

Haul trucks are used for mining and heavy-duty construction jobs. One of the biggest haul trucks in the world is almost 27 feet high and can carry over 1 million pounds of material – that's taller than an adult giraffe and heavier than the combined weight of four blue whales.

AMBULANCE

Ambulances are emergency vehicles used for transporting injured and sick people to the hospital. As early as 900 CE, carts with hammocks were used for this purpose. Modern ambulances have specialist medical equipment, ramps, sirens, flashing lights, and radios for following traffic news.

FORKLIFT

Forklifts are used in warehouses and factories all over the world to load and move heavy boxes. These vehicles save businesses huge amounts of time and money — without them, workers would have to move the boxes themselves, which would take longer and risk causing injuries.

TELESCOPIC HANDLER

A telescopic handler works in a similar way to a forklift truck but can reach higher. It can hold heavy loads with its fork-like attachment and then lift them up to a high point using its extendable "boom" arm.

ROAD TRAIN

A road train is used to transport goods as quickly as possible across rural and remote areas in Australia, primarily, but also the United States and Europe. Some of Australia's road trains are so big that they are only allowed to drive in the remote Outback regions.

DID YOU KNOW?

The longest journey ever made by tractor is about 15,769 miles. The driver was Hubert Berger, from Germany. Hubert's journey took him to 36 different countries across Europe.

BACKHOE LOADER

On a backhoe loader, there is a boom, a stick, and a digging bucket mounted on to the back of the truck. These parts are connected to each other by joints, like in your arm. They work together to dig, lift, and dump material.

PICKUP TRUCK

The pickup truck was originally used only for practical jobs, with its open cargo area perfect for carrying different tools and equipment. Since the 1950s, however, the trucks have also become a popular car replacement, with people using them for everyday activities.

SNOWPLOW

Snowplows were invented in Norway to clear thick snow and ice from roads and railway tracks. When snowfall is particularly heavy, snowplows clear routes for emergency vehicles first.

CEMENT MIXER

A cement mixer makes concrete by mixing cement and water with sand or gravel in a drum. The truck carefully transports the liquid concrete to building sites, where it is then unloaded down a chute.

SKID-STEER LOADER

Skid-steer loaders are small machines used on building sites to lift, dig, and dump different materials. The truck's arms can be fitted with an amazing range of attachments, including a concrete crusher, a wood chipper, and a digger.

ROADHEADER

Roadheaders are impressive machines with powerful, turning cutter heads. They drill into rock faces to create tunnels, and into the ground to create mines.

TRUCK-MOUNTED DRILL

Drilling rigs are used to drill holes into Earth's surface to create wells for oil and water. Larger rigs are built as permanent structures – either in the ground or in the middle of the ocean. Smaller, mobile rigs are mounted on to trucks.

SKIP LOADER

Over 200 million tons of trash is thrown away every year, and much of this waste goes into skips. Skip loaders are designed specially for carrying and moving these skips to places where the waste can be sorted through properly.

FACE-SHOVEL EXCAVATOR

Face-shovel excavators have large buckets that dig material and dump it into a haul truck or dumper truck. Face-shovels are strong and speedy workers, shifting weights of over 230,000 pounds in a single scoop — that's 17 times heavier than a *Tyrannosaurus rex*.

BAGGAGE TRUCK

A baggage truck is one of the many vehicles you might spot on an airport runway. They carry luggage from the terminal building to the airplane, transporting millions of bags each year.

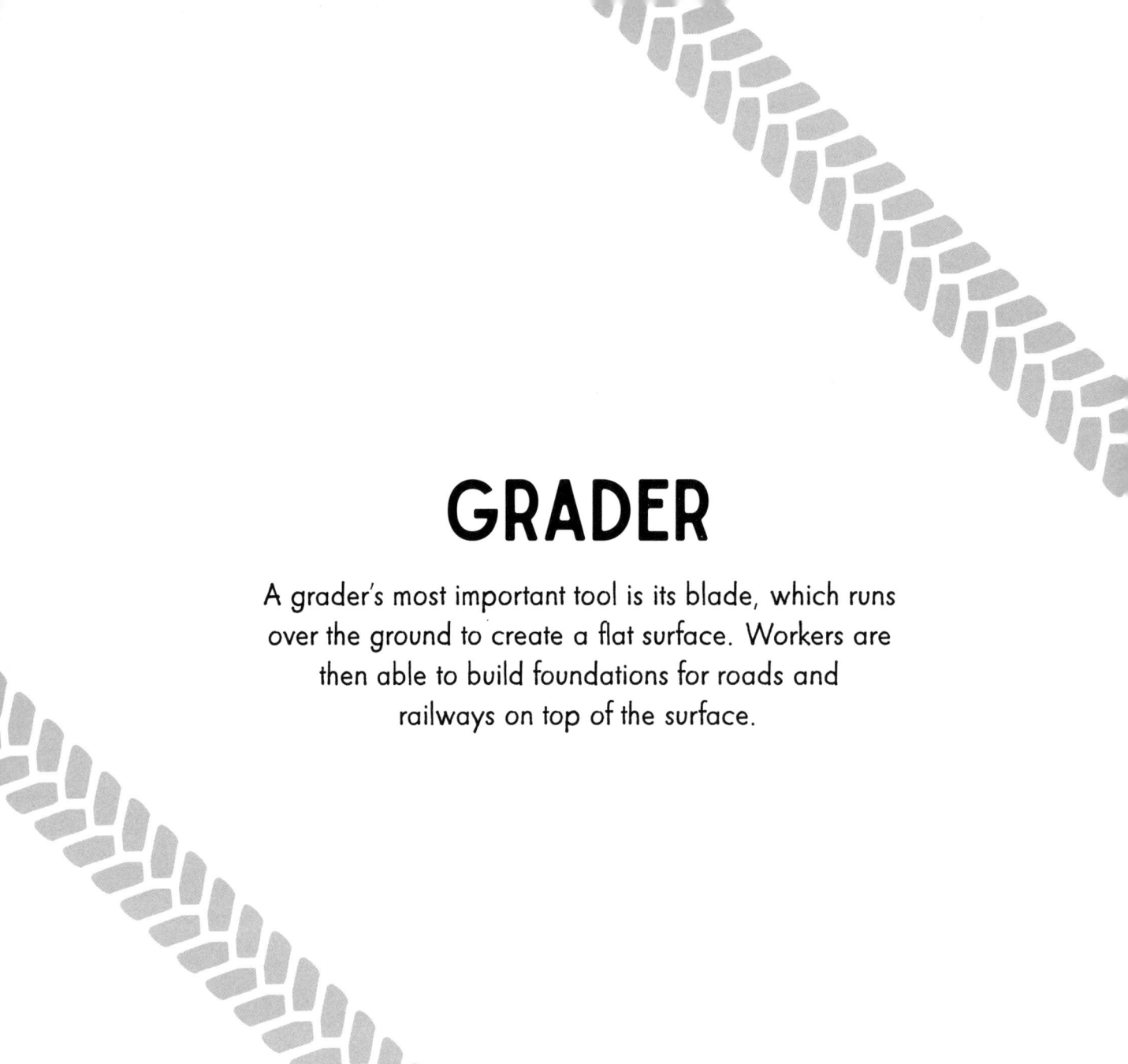

GRADER

A grader's most important tool is its blade, which runs over the ground to create a flat surface. Workers are then able to build foundations for roads and railways on top of the surface.